D1175883

UNLEASH THE **WOLF WITHIN**

ISBN-979-8-9876794-1-8

Designed by Olori Swank
Published by SWANK Universe Inc.

Printed in USA

For details or ordering information, contact the publisher at info@swankuniverse.com

THIS JOURNAL BELONGS TO

_____

# INTRODUCTION

Welcome to "Unleash the Wolf Within: A 30-Day Journal for Motivation, Inspiration, and Personal Growth"! This journal is designed to help you tap into your full potential and unlock the power of self-care, mindfulness, and positive thinking. It will guide you on a journey of self-discovery, where you will learn to cultivate a growth mindset, build resilience, and manifest the life you truly want.

This journal is for anyone who is feeling uninspired and struggling with a lack of motivation. It's for those who feel lost and are in need of finding themselves again, discovering their purpose, and reawakening their inner beast. It's a powerful tool that will help you to break free from limiting beliefs and self-doubt and discover your true potential.

Each day, you will be presented with new challenges and opportunities to learn, grow, and transform. You will find powerful exercises and activities that will help you to develop a growth mindset, build resilience, and manifest the life you truly want. You will also find guided journaling prompts that will help you to reflect on your progress and understand yourself better.

The journal also includes an appendix of worksheets that will help you to understand and track your progress, as well as 30 days of inspirational affirmations to keep you motivated and inspired. By the end of this journal, you will have a better understanding of yourself, your strengths, and your purpose. You will have the tools and knowledge necessary to create the life you truly want, and you will have a deeper appreciation for self-care, mindfulness, and positive thinking.

# INTRODUCTION

Before you begin, it's important to set your intentions for this journey. Take some time to reflect on what you hope to achieve and what you want to change. This journal is your guide, your companion and your tool; it's up to you to take action, be consistent and commit to the process. Remember that change takes time and effort, but with dedication and consistency, you can achieve your goals. This journal is not just about writing, it's about taking action and making meaningful changes in your life. So, take a deep breath, trust the process and let's begin this journey together. Unleash the Wolf Within and discover your true potential.

# SETTING YOUR INTENTIONS

Before you begin this journal, it's important to take some time to reflect on your intentions for this journey. Setting clear intentions will help you to stay focused and motivated as you work through the exercises and activities in the journal.

Here are some steps to help you set your intentions:

1. Take a moment to reflect on where you are currently in your life. What are your strengths and weaknesses? What are your goals and aspirations?
2. Identify the areas of your life that you want to improve. This could be anything from your career, relationships, health, or personal growth.
3. Set specific and measurable goals for yourself. For example, if you want to improve your health, set a goal to exercise for 30 minutes a day, or if you want to improve your relationships, set a goal to have a meaningful conversation with a loved one at least once a week.
4. Write down your intentions. Write down your goals and aspirations, and be as specific as possible. This will help you to stay focused and motivated throughout the journal.
5. Reflect on your intentions daily. Take a moment each day to reflect on your intentions and the progress you've made towards achieving them.
6. Review and adjust your intentions as you go. Remember that your intentions and goals may change as you work through the journal, and that's okay. Be open to adjusting your intentions as you learn and grow.

By setting clear and specific intentions, you will be able to stay focused and motivated throughout your journey. Remember to be kind and compassionate with yourself as you work through the journal, and always keep in mind that progress takes time and effort, but with dedication and consistency, you can achieve your goals.

# HOW TO USE THE JOURNAL

1. Set aside time each day to work on the journal. We recommend setting aside at least 15-30 minutes each day to complete the exercises, activities, and journaling prompts.
2. Follow the journal in order. The journal is designed to be completed in order, with each day building on the previous one.
3. Be honest and open. The journal is a safe space for self-reflection and self-discovery. Be honest with yourself as you work through the exercises and activities, and be open to new ideas and perspectives.
4. Customize the journal to suit your needs. Feel free to adapt the exercises and activities to suit your individual needs and preferences.
5. Reflect on your progress. Take the time to reflect on your progress and your intentions throughout the journal. This will help you to stay motivated and on track.
6. Use the additional resources in the appendix. The appendix includes helpful tools such as the Habit Tracker, Daily Manifest, Life Inventory, and Bucket List. These resources can be used to supplement the journal and help you to understand and track your progress.
7. Keep the journal for future reference. This journal is a valuable tool for self-reflection and self-discovery. Keep it for future reference and refer back to it whenever you need to.
8. Be consistent. Remember that change takes time and effort, but with dedication and consistency, you can achieve your goals.

This journal is designed to be user-friendly, flexible and adaptable to the user's needs. It is a valuable tool for self-discovery, personal growth and motivation. The journal is filled with daily activities, exercises, and journaling prompts that will guide you on a journey of self-discovery. The additional resources in the appendix are there to support and supplement the journal. Remember that consistency and dedication are key to achieving progress and reaching your goals.

# UNLEASH THE **WOLF WITHIN**

| 1 Discovering Your Purpose | 2 Building Self-Awareness | 3 Overcoming Limiting Beliefs | 4 Cultivating a Growth Mindset | 5 Setting Goals |
|---|---|---|---|---|
| 6 Mindful Movement | 7 Reflecting on the Week | 8 Building Resilience | 9 Embracing Self-Care | 10 Mindful Eating |
| 11 Connecting with Nature | 12 Mindful Communication | 13 Reflecting on the Week | 14 The Power of Positive Thinking | 15 Practicing Gratitude |
| 16 Mindful Listening | 17 Mindful Walking | 18 Connecting with Others | 19 Reflecting on the Week | 20 Manifesting Your Dreams |
| 21 Mindful Cooking | 22 Mindful Reading | 23 Mindful Puzzle Solving | 24 Reflecting on the Week | 25 Embracing Self-Compassion |
| 26 Creating a Vision Board | 27 Identifying and Overcoming Fears | 28 Reflecting on Progress | 29 Self-Affirmations | 30 Reflecting on Your Journey |

**30 DAYS AT A GLANCE**

# DAY 1: DISCOVERING YOUR PURPOSE

**AFFIRMATION:**

I am clear on my purpose and know that I am making a positive impact in the world.

- Write about your current understanding of your purpose in life. What is important to you? What values drive you?

- Reflect on past experiences and moments in your life when you felt most fulfilled. What were you doing? Who were you with? How can you incorporate more of these experiences into your daily life?

_____
_____
_____
_____
_____
_____
_____
_____
_____
_____
_____
_____
_____
_____
_____

# DAY 2: BUILDING SELF-AWARENESS

**AFFIRMATION:**

I am becoming more self-aware every day and am able to understand my thoughts and emotions.

- Take a few minutes to sit in silence and observe your thoughts and emotions without judgment. Write down any patterns or themes that you notice.

- Reflect on your strengths and weaknesses. What are you naturally good at? What do you struggle with? How can you use this knowledge to improve yourself?

_____

_____

_____

_____

_____

_____

_____

_____

_____

_____

_____

_____

_____

_____

_____

_____

_____

UNLEASH THE **WOLF WITHIN**

# SELF ASSESSMENT

Unlock the power within yourself to reach new heights of well-being by utilizing this assessment tool. Take a deep dive into your physical, emotional, spiritual, and professional self and discover areas for growth. And as you complete the assessment, take the opportunity to jot down the areas you wish to improve and the steps you plan to take to achieve that growth.

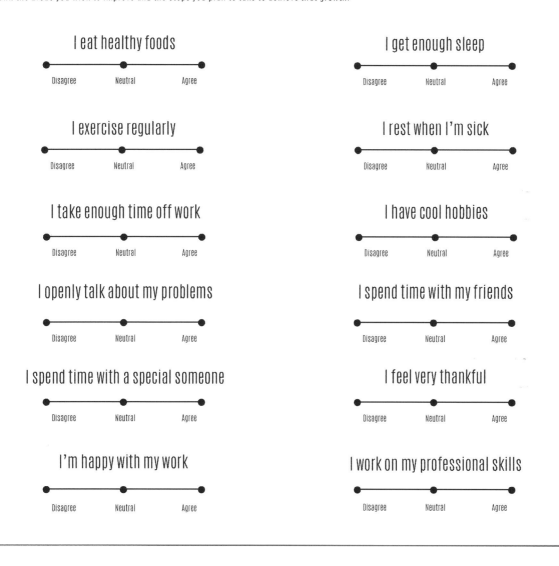

### I eat healthy foods
Disagree    Neutral    Agree

### I get enough sleep
Disagree    Neutral    Agree

### I exercise regularly
Disagree    Neutral    Agree

### I rest when I'm sick
Disagree    Neutral    Agree

### I take enough time off work
Disagree    Neutral    Agree

### I have cool hobbies
Disagree    Neutral    Agree

### I openly talk about my problems
Disagree    Neutral    Agree

### I spend time with my friends
Disagree    Neutral    Agree

### I spend time with a special someone
Disagree    Neutral    Agree

### I feel very thankful
Disagree    Neutral    Agree

### I'm happy with my work
Disagree    Neutral    Agree

### I work on my professional skills
Disagree    Neutral    Agree

What would I like to improve and how:

# DAY 3: OVERCOMING LIMITING BELIEFS

**AFFIRMATION:**

I am strong and capable of overcoming any limiting beliefs that hold me back.

- Write down any limiting beliefs that you currently have about yourself. For example, "I'm not good enough," "I'll never be successful," "I'm not attractive."

- Challenge these beliefs by writing evidence to the contrary. For example, "I've accomplished X, Y, and Z in my life."

# LIMITING BELIEFS

Use this page to uncover and overcome limiting beliefs that are holding you back. Take the opportunity to reframe them into empowering thoughts that will drive you towards success. For example, instead of believing that "money does not grow on trees," shift your mindset to "I will be rewarded for the value I provide for others. The more I give, the more I will receive."

Current Belief

Better Alternative

Current Belief

Better Alternative

Current Belief

Better Alternative

Current Belief

Better Alternative

# DAY 4: CULTIVATING A GROWTH MINDSET

**AFFIRMATION:**

I am open to learning and growing, and embrace challenges as opportunities for growth.

- Reflect on a recent setback or challenge that you faced. Write down what you learned from the experience and how you can apply that lesson to future situations.

- Write down one specific goal that you have for yourself and how a growth mindset can help you achieve it.

_____
_____
_____
_____
_____
_____
_____
_____
_____
_____
_____
_____
_____
_____
_____

UNLEASH THE **WOLF WITHIN**

# GROWTH VS FIXED MINDSET

---

Unlock your full potential and achieve your goals by embracing a growth mindset! According to researcher Carol Dweck, a simple shift in mindset can lead to remarkable progress. Say goodbye to the limiting belief of a fixed mindset and embrace the power of continuous improvement. Remember that with a growth mindset, you have the power to improve any quality with effort and determination. Take a look at the examples below to see the difference between a fixed and growth mindset and choose to empower yourself with a growth mindset .

| GROWTH MINDSET | FIXED MINDSET |
|:---:|:---:|
| **Challenges** | **Challenges** |
| Challenges are a way for me to get better | I try to avoid challenges so I don't look stupid |
| **Desires** | **Desires** |
| I'll try new things | I'll just stick to what I know |
| **Skills** | **Skills** |
| I can always improve | I'm either good at it or not. If I'm not, it's okay |
| **Obstacles** | **Obstacles** |
| I'll change my approach until I succeed | I'm just not good at it and that's the way it is |
| **Success of Others** | **Success of Others** |
| I'm inspired by their success. Maybe I have something to learn from their success. | It's unfair that they're succeeding and I am not. |
| **Criticism** | **Criticism** |
| I can learn from the feedback I receive | I feel threatened by the criticism I get |

# DAY 5: SETTING GOALS

- Reflect on your long-term vision for your life. What do you want to achieve? Who do you want to be?

- Break that long-term vision into smaller, specific, and measurable goals that you can work on each day.

_____
_____
_____
_____
_____
_____
_____
_____
_____
_____
_____
_____
_____
_____
_____

# GOAL SETTING

---

## MY VISION OR GOAL:

ex. build a 6 figure passion business in the next two years.

## STEPS TO TAKE:

ex. building a brand around my expertise

## FINANCIAL COST:

ex. hiring freelancers

## ACTIONS TO TAKE:

ex. building out my portfolio website

## POTENTIAL PROBLEMS:

ex. saturated marketplace,
how will you differentiate?

## PROGRESS TRACKER:

what have I done already
to achieve my goal

# DAY 6: MINDFUL MOVEMENT

**AFFIRMATION:**

I take care of my physical and mental well-being through mindful movement and exercise.

- Take 10-15 minutes to engage in any form of physical movement that you enjoy, such as yoga, walking, or dancing. As you move, focus on the sensation of your body and breathe deeply.

- Write down how you felt before and after the movement. How did your body and mind feel? How do you feel now?

_____
_____
_____
_____
_____
_____
_____
_____
_____
_____
_____
_____
_____
_____
_____

# DAY 7: REFLECTING ON THE WEEK

**AFFIRMATION:**

I reflect on my progress and growth, and make plans for continued improvement.

- Reflect on the past week. What did you learn? What did you accomplish? What could you have done better?

- Write down any plans or intentions for the next week.

_____

_____

_____

_____

_____

_____

_____

_____

_____

_____

_____

_____

_____

_____

_____

_____

# DAY 8: BUILDING RESILIENCE

**AFFIRMATION:**

I am strong and resilient, and I bounce back from challenges and adversity.

- Reflect on a time when you faced a difficult challenge and overcame it. Write about what you did to stay strong and what you learned from the experience.

- Identify one specific step you can take today to build your resilience in the face of future challenges.

_____
_____
_____
_____
_____
_____
_____
_____
_____
_____
_____
_____
_____
_____
_____
_____

# DAY 9: EMBRACING SELF-CARE

**AFFIRMATION:**

I take care of myself physically, mentally, and emotionally, and prioritize my well-being.

- Reflect on your current self-care routine. What do you do to take care of yourself physically, emotionally, and mentally? What works well for you? What doesn't work well for you?

- Identify one specific step you can take today to prioritize self-care in your life.

_____
_____
_____
_____
_____
_____
_____
_____
_____
_____
_____
_____
_____
_____
_____

UNLEASH THE **WOLF WITHIN**

# DAY 10: MINDFUL EATING

**AFFIRMATION:**

I make mindful and healthy food choices, and appreciate the nourishment my body receives.

- Take a few minutes to focus on your breath before starting your meal. As you eat, pay attention to the taste, texture, and temperature of your food. Chew slowly and savor each bite.

- Reflect on how you felt before, during, and after your meal. How was your hunger and fullness levels? How did your body feel?

_____

_____

_____

_____

_____

_____

_____

_____

_____

_____

_____

_____

_____

_____

# DAY 11: CONNECTING WITH NATURE

**AFFIRMATION:**

I connect with nature and find peace and tranquility in the natural world.

- Take a 10-15 minute walk outside. As you walk, focus on your surroundings. Notice the colors, textures, and shapes of the natural environment.

- Reflect on your experience afterwards. How did being in nature make you feel? What can you take from this experience and apply to your daily life?

_____

_____

_____

_____

_____

_____

_____

_____

_____

_____

_____

_____

_____

_____

UNLEASH THE **WOLF WITHIN**

# DAY 12: MINDFUL COMMUNICATION

**AFFIRMATION:**

I communicate mindfully and effectively, and listen actively to others.

- Reflect on a recent communication experience where you felt frustrated or misunderstood. Write down what happened, how you felt, and what could have been done differently.

- Identify one specific step you can take today to improve your communication skills, such as active listening or expressing yourself clearly.

_____

_____

_____

_____

_____

_____

_____

_____

_____

_____

_____

_____

_____

_____

_____

_____

# DAY 13: REFLECTING ON THE WEEK

## AFFIRMATION:

I reflect on my progress and growth, and make plans for continued improvement.

- Reflect on the past week. What did you learn? What did you accomplish? What could you have done better?

- Write down any plans or intentions for the next week.

_____
_____
_____
_____
_____
_____
_____
_____
_____
_____
_____
_____
_____
_____
_____

UNLEASH THE **WOLF WITHIN**

# DAY 14: HARNESSING THE POWER OF POSITIVE THINKING

**AFFIRMATION:**

I choose to focus on the positive and believe in the power of my thoughts to shape my reality.

- Reflect on any negative thoughts or self-talk that you've had recently. Write them down.

- Challenge those negative thoughts by writing a more positive and realistic perspective.

_____
_____
_____
_____
_____
_____
_____
_____
_____
_____
_____
_____
_____
_____

# DAY 15: PRACTICING GRATITUDE

**AFFIRMATION:**

I am grateful for all the blessings in my life and focus on the good in every situation.

- Write down three things you are grateful for today. It can be big or small things.

- Reflect on how expressing gratitude made you feel. How does it change your perspective on things?

_____
_____
_____
_____
_____
_____
_____
_____
_____
_____
_____
_____
_____
_____
_____

# GRATITUDE WORKSHEET

Make a list of your most recent positive experiences and the little things you can be grateful for. The purpose of this exercise is to make yourself appreciate all the good things that are happening that you otherwise might just overlook.

## TODAY I'M GRATEFUL FOR:

☐ _____

☐ _____

☐ _____

☐ _____

☐ _____

## PEOPLE I'M GRATEFUL FOR:

☐ _____

☐ _____

☐ _____

☐ _____

☐ _____

## SOMETHING AWESOME THAT HAPPENED:

☐ _____

☐ _____

☐ _____

☐ _____

☐ _____

## MY BEST MEMORIES:

☐ _____

☐ _____

☐ _____

☐ _____

☐ _____

## BEST PARTS OF MY DAY:

☐ _____

☐ _____

☐ _____

☐ _____

☐ _____

## THINGS THAT MADE ME SMILE:

☐ _____

☐ _____

☐ _____

☐ _____

☐ _____

# DAY 16: MINDFUL LISTENING

**AFFIRMATION:**

I listen actively and attentively to others, and communicate with empathy and understanding.

- Reflect on a recent conversation where you were not fully present or attentive. Write down what happened, how you felt and what you could have done differently.

- Set an intention for your next conversation to be fully present and listen attentively.

_____

_____

_____

_____

_____

_____

_____

_____

_____

_____

_____

_____

_____

_____

_____

# DAY 17: MINDFUL WALKING

**AFFIRMATION:**

I take mindful walks to clear my mind, connect with nature and focus on the present moment.

- Take a 10-15 minute walk. As you walk, focus on your surroundings and your breath. Let go of any distracting thoughts or worries.

- Reflect on how you felt before and after the walk. How does your body and mind feel? How does this compare to a regular walk?

UNLEASH THE **WOLF WITHIN**

# DAY 18: CONNECTING WITH OTHERS

**AFFIRMATION:**

I am surrounded by love and support.

- Reflect on your current relationships and social connections. Who do you have in your life that you are grateful for? Who do you want to connect with more?

- Identify one specific step you can take today to strengthen your relationships and build new connections.

_____
_____
_____
_____
_____
_____
_____
_____
_____
_____
_____
_____
_____
_____
_____
_____

# MY RELATIONSHIPS

Take control of your relationships and chart a path towards fulfilling connections by utilizing this section. Rate your current relationships on a scale of 1 to 10 and reflect on what makes them important to you. In each box, take the opportunity to celebrate what you're happy with and identify areas for growth. Consider how these relationships are supporting you on your journey towards the life you're striving to create.

## RELATIONSHIP

| 01 | 02 | 03 | 04 | 05 | 06 | 07 | 08 | 09 | 10 |
|----|----|----|----|----|----|----|----|----|----|

What are you happy with & what to improve

## RELATIONSHIP

| 01 | 02 | 03 | 04 | 05 | 06 | 07 | 08 | 09 | 10 |
|----|----|----|----|----|----|----|----|----|----|

What are you happy with & what to improve

## RELATIONSHIP

| 01 | 02 | 03 | 04 | 05 | 06 | 07 | 08 | 09 | 10 |
|----|----|----|----|----|----|----|----|----|----|

What are you happy with & what to improve

## RELATIONSHIP

| 01 | 02 | 03 | 04 | 05 | 06 | 07 | 08 | 09 | 10 |
|----|----|----|----|----|----|----|----|----|----|

What are you happy with & what to improve

UNLEASH THE **WOLF WITHIN**

# MY RELATIONSHIPS

Take control of your relationships and chart a path towards fulfilling connections by utilizing this section. Rate your current relationships on a scale of 1 to 10 and reflect on what makes them important to you. In each box, take the opportunity to celebrate what you're happy with and identify areas for growth. Consider how these relationships are supporting you on your journey towards the life you're striving to create.

## RELATIONSHIP

| 01 | 02 | 03 | 04 | 05 | 06 | 07 | 08 | 09 | 10 |
|----|----|----|----|----|----|----|----|----|----|

What are you happy with & what to improve

## RELATIONSHIP

| 01 | 02 | 03 | 04 | 05 | 06 | 07 | 08 | 09 | 10 |
|----|----|----|----|----|----|----|----|----|----|

What are you happy with & what to improve

## RELATIONSHIP

| 01 | 02 | 03 | 04 | 05 | 06 | 07 | 08 | 09 | 10 |
|----|----|----|----|----|----|----|----|----|----|

What are you happy with & what to improve

## RELATIONSHIP

| 01 | 02 | 03 | 04 | 05 | 06 | 07 | 08 | 09 | 10 |
|----|----|----|----|----|----|----|----|----|----|

What are you happy with & what to improve

## UNLEASH THE **WOLF WITHIN**

# DAY 19: REFLECTING ON THE WEEK

**AFFIRMATION:**

I reflect on my progress and growth, and make plans for continued improvement.

- Reflect on the past week. What did you learn? What did you accomplish? What could you have done better?

- Write down any plans or intentions for the next week.

# DAY 20: MANIFESTING YOUR DREAMS

**AFFIRMATION:**

I believe in my ability to manifest my dreams and take action towards making them a reality.

- Reflect on your long-term vision for your life. What do you want to achieve? Who do you want to be?

- Identify one specific step you can take today to bring you closer to manifesting your dreams.

_____
_____
_____
_____
_____
_____
_____
_____
_____
_____
_____
_____
_____

# DAY 21: MINDFUL COOKING

## AFFIRMATION:

I cook with intention and mindfulness, creating delicious and healthy meals for myself and loved ones.

- Take your time to prepare a meal, focusing on each step of the process. Smell and taste the ingredients, pay attention to the textures and colors, and enjoy the process of creating something delicious.

- Reflect on how you felt before, during, and after the cooking process.

# DAY 22: MINDFUL READING

## AFFIRMATION:

I read with intention and mindfulness, gaining knowledge and inspiration to enhance my personal growth.

- Pick a book or article to read. As you read, focus on the words and their meanings. Take your time to really absorb the material.

- Reflect on how you felt before, during, and after reading. How does this compare to your usual reading experience?

_____
_____
_____
_____
_____
_____
_____
_____
_____
_____
_____
_____
_____
_____
_____
_____

# DAY 23: MINDFUL PUZZLE SOLVING

**AFFIRMATION:**

I engage in mindful activities to challenge my mind, improve my focus and boost my problem-solving skills.

- Take time to work on a puzzle, whether it's a jigsaw puzzle, Sudoku, or crossword. As you work, focus on the task at hand and let go of any distracting thoughts or worries.

- Reflect on how you felt before, during, and after solving the puzzle. How does this compare to your usual puzzle solving experience?

_____
_____
_____
_____
_____
_____
_____
_____
_____
_____
_____
_____
_____
_____
_____
_____

# DAY 24: REFLECTING ON THE WEEK

**AFFIRMATION:**

I reflect on my progress and growth, and make plans for continued improvement.

- Reflect on the past week. What did you learn? What did you accomplish? What could you have done better?

- Write down any plans or intentions for the next week.

_____

_____

_____

_____

_____

_____

_____

_____

_____

_____

_____

_____

_____

_____

_____

_____

UNLEASH THE **WOLF WITHIN**

# DAY 25: EMBRACING SELF-COMPASSION

**AFFIRMATION:**

I am kind and compassionate towards myself, and practice self-care and self-love.

- Reflect on any negative thoughts or self-talk that you've had recently. Write them down.

- Challenge those negative thoughts by writing a more positive and realistic perspective.

_____

_____

_____

_____

_____

_____

_____

_____

_____

_____

_____

_____

_____

_____

_____

_____

# DAY 26: CREATING A VISION BOARD

**AFFIRMATION:**

I visualize my goals and aspirations, and take steps towards making them a reality.

- Reflect on your long-term goals and aspirations. Identify specific images, words, and phrases that represent these goals and aspirations.

- Create a vision board using these images, words, and phrases as a visual reminder of what you are working towards.

# VISION BOARD

Unleash your full potential and bring your dream life to reality by writing down key points in each category that describe your ideal life. This page is your opportunity to paint a vivid picture of what you want to achieve, and putting your vision in writing will make it more tangible and real. Don't underestimate the power of writing - it creates a commitment that drives you forward towards your goals.

| CAREER | FINANCE |
|---|---|
| | |
| **RELATIONSHIPS** | **LOVE** |
| | |
| **PERSONAL GROWTH** | **HEALTH** |
| | |
| **LEISURE** | **HOME** |
| | |

# DAY 27: IDENTIFYING AND OVERCOMING FEARS

**AFFIRMATION:**

I identify and overcome my fears, and take steps towards achieving my goals.

- Reflect on any fears or limiting beliefs that are holding you back from achieving your goals.

- Identify one specific step you can take today to overcome or work through this fear.

_____
_____
_____
_____
_____
_____
_____
_____
_____
_____
_____
_____
_____
_____
_____
_____

UNLEASH THE **WOLF WITHIN**

# FEAR SETTING

---

Unleash your full potential and conquer your fears by taking part in this transformative exercise, inspired by Tim Ferriss's "4 Hour Work Week". Face your fears head on and imagine the worst possible outcomes of an action you know you need to take. By breaking down the challenges into three categories: worst outcomes, prevention, and mitigation, you'll see that the things you're afraid of are not as daunting as they seem. And if that's not enough motivation, think about the long-term consequences of inaction to push yourself towards taking bold, courageous action. Embrace this exercise and transform your fears into opportunities.

WHAT ACTION DO YOU WISH TO TAKE

| THE WORST OUTCOMES | HOW TO PREVENT | HOW TO REPAIR |
|---|---|---|
| | | |

WHAT WILL HAPPEN LONG TERM (1 YEAR, 5 YEARS, 10 YEARS+) IF YOU DON'T TAKE THIS ACTION?

# DAY 28: REFLECTING ON PROGRESS

## AFFIRMATION:

I am proud of my progress and take steps to continue growing and improving.

- Reflect on your progress over the past month. What have you accomplished? What has changed?

- Write down any plans or intentions for continuing your personal growth and development.

_____
_____
_____
_____
_____
_____
_____
_____
_____
_____
_____
_____
_____
_____
_____
_____

# DAY 29: SELF-AFFIRMATIONS

**AFFIRMATION:**

I speak positively to myself and believe in my abilities.

- Reflect on any negative self-talk or beliefs that you have about yourself. Write them down.

- Create a list of positive affirmations that counteract these negative beliefs, and make it a practice to repeat them to yourself throughout the day.

_____

_____

_____

_____

_____

_____

_____

_____

_____

_____

_____

_____

_____

_____

_____

_____

UNLEASH THE **WOLF WITHIN**

# AFFIRMATIONS

In this part, you'll have the opportunity to write down affirmations that will have a transformative impact on the aspects of your life you're striving to improve. Remember to always write in present tense using the "I" pronoun, choose affirmative and positive words, and make a habit of using your affirmations when you need a boost of motivation. For example "I'm full of energy and always take action", instead of "I'm not lazy". Take control of your thoughts and beliefs and unleash your full potential with the power of positive affirmations.

## RELATIONSHIPS

ex. "I'm loving and giving in my relationships". "I'm in control of the people I let in my life"

## FINANCE

ex. "I'm capable of creating my dream financial life through hard work and dedication"

## CAREER

ex. "I'm always striving to develop myself professionally"

## HEALTH/FITNESS

ex. "I'm in control of my physical fitness"

## LOVE

ex. "I have people who love me"

# DAY 30: REFLECTING ON YOUR JOURNEY

**AFFIRMATION:**

I am proud of my personal growth and the progress I've made on my journey.

- Reflect on your journey over the past 30 days. How have you grown? What have you learned about yourself?

- Write down your next steps and intentions for continuing your personal growth and development.

UNLEASH THE **WOLF WITHIN**

# CONCLUSION

Congratulations on completing "Unleash the Wolf Within: A 30-Day Journal for Motivation, Inspiration, and Personal Growth"! This journal has been a journey of self-discovery, personal growth, and motivation.

You have worked through powerful exercises, activities, affirmations, and guided journaling prompts that have helped you to discover your purpose, overcome obstacles, and achieve your goals.
You have learned to tap into your full potential, unlock the power of self-care, mindfulness, and positive thinking. You have cultivated a growth mindset, built resilience, and manifested the life you truly want. You have a better understanding of yourself, your strengths, and your purpose.

As you look back on the journal, take time to reflect on your progress and the changes that you have made. Remember that change takes time and effort, but with dedication and consistency, you can achieve your goals. You have the tools and knowledge to continue to create the life you truly want.

This is not the end of your journey, it is only the beginning. This journal is your companion, your guide, and your tool, and you can always refer back to it whenever you need inspiration, motivation, or guidance. Remember to always be kind and compassionate with yourself, and to continue to practice self-care, mindfulness, and positive thinking.

# ACKNOWLEDGMENTS

Writing this journal has been a journey, and I couldn't have done it without the support and guidance of many people in my life.

First and foremost, I would like to thank my family for their unwavering support and encouragement throughout this process. Their love and encouragement has been a constant source of inspiration.

I am also grateful to my friends who have been my sounding board, my cheerleaders, and my confidantes throughout this journey. They have been my support system and I couldn't have done it without them.

I would like to express my deep gratitude to the experts, healers and speakers who have contributed their knowledge to this journal; their works and teachings have been a valuable source of information.

I would also like to acknowledge and thank the many members of my online community that have provided support and positive vibes throughout this process.

Finally, I would like to thank you, the reader, for choosing this journal and embarking on this journey with me. I hope that it has been a valuable tool for self-discovery, personal growth, and motivation.

Thank you all for your support, guidance, and encouragement.

With Love,


Olori Swank

# APPENDIX

UNLEASH THE **WOLF WITHIN**

# LIFE INVENTORY

Take a moment to evaluate your current circumstances across different areas of your life and assign each a score from 1 to 10. A score of 1 represents unhappiness with the present state and 10 represents complete contentment. This exercise provides valuable insights into what you need to focus on and make improvements in. Jot down what you cherish about your current situation and what steps you can take to enhance it. Celebrate your progress by repeating this exercise every six months and marvel at the growth you've made!

**RELATIONSHIPS**

| 01 | 02 | 03 | 04 | 05 | 06 | 07 | 08 | 09 | 10 |
|----|----|----|----|----|----|----|----|----|----|

**FINANCE**

| 01 | 02 | 03 | 04 | 05 | 06 | 07 | 08 | 09 | 10 |
|----|----|----|----|----|----|----|----|----|----|

**CAREER**

| 01 | 02 | 03 | 04 | 05 | 06 | 07 | 08 | 09 | 10 |
|----|----|----|----|----|----|----|----|----|----|

**HEALTH/FITNESS**

| 01 | 02 | 03 | 04 | 05 | 06 | 07 | 08 | 09 | 10 |
|----|----|----|----|----|----|----|----|----|----|

**RECREATION**

| 01 | 02 | 03 | 04 | 05 | 06 | 07 | 08 | 09 | 10 |
|----|----|----|----|----|----|----|----|----|----|

# MY IDEAL LIFE

Imagine waking up each day filled with purpose and excitement, surrounded by the people and experiences that bring you joy. Visualize your mornings, evenings, and nights filled with activities and experiences that bring you fulfillment. Dream of a professional life that aligns with your passions and values. Remember, this is just the beginning of your journey, and your vision may evolve and grow as you move forward.

_____

_____

_____

_____

_____

_____

_____

_____

_____

_____

_____

_____

_____

_____

_____

_____

_____

_____

_____

_____

_____

_____

# THINGS I WANT

This is your chance to let your imagination soar! Write down everything you desire in life - from a stunning new home to a yearly adventure in a tropical paradise. Don't hold back - dream big! Beside each item, estimate the cost and discover that you don't have to be a millionaire to have everything you want in life (depending on your desires, of course). The power of this exercise is to put your dreams in writing and use them as a source of motivation and drive.

## ITEM NAME

## EST. COST

01

02

03

04

05

06

07

08

09

10

11

12

13

14

15

16

17

18

19

20

# BUCKET LIST

## ACHIEVEMENTS

On this side, write down all the things you want to ACHIEVE in your life - physically, financially, relationship-wise, in your career, etc.

## EXPERIENCES

On this side, write down all the things you want to EXPERIENCE in your life - happiness, new places, foods etc.

# ACTION BRAINSTORM

| STOP DOING | |
| DO LESS | |
| KEEP DOING | |
| DO MORE | |
| START DOING | |

# HABIT TRACKER

| | READ | JOURNAL | MEDITATE | WORK OUT | FAMILY TIME | EAT CLEAN | | | | |
|----|------|---------|----------|----------|-------------|-----------|---|---|---|---|
| 01 | | | | | | | | | | |
| 02 | | | | | | | | | | |
| 03 | | | | | | | | | | |
| 04 | | | | | | | | | | |
| 05 | | | | | | | | | | |
| 06 | | | | | | | | | | |
| 07 | | | | | | | | | | |
| 08 | | | | | | | | | | |
| 09 | | | | | | | | | | |
| 10 | | | | | | | | | | |
| 11 | | | | | | | | | | |
| 12 | | | | | | | | | | |
| 13 | | | | | | | | | | |
| 14 | | | | | | | | | | |
| 15 | | | | | | | | | | |
| 16 | | | | | | | | | | |
| 17 | | | | | | | | | | |
| 18 | | | | | | | | | | |
| 19 | | | | | | | | | | |
| 20 | | | | | | | | | | |
| 21 | | | | | | | | | | |
| 22 | | | | | | | | | | |
| 23 | | | | | | | | | | |
| 24 | | | | | | | | | | |
| 25 | | | | | | | | | | |
| 26 | | | | | | | | | | |
| 27 | | | | | | | | | | |
| 28 | | | | | | | | | | |
| 29 | | | | | | | | | | |
| 30 | | | | | | | | | | |
| 31 | | | | | | | | | | |

# DAILY MANIFEST

DATE:

## DAILY PRIORITIES

Give direction to your daily tasks - Write down what you want to achieve during the day and why it is important to you. Think long term - How are these things going to help you in 1 month, 6 months, or 1 year? If they won't, chances are, they're not that important.

**01**
_____
_____
_____
_____
_____

**02**
_____
_____
_____
_____
_____

**03**
_____
_____
_____
_____
_____

## TO-DO LIST

Less important things to get done during the day. These might not be that strategic long term, but need to be done nevertheless.

**01** _____
**02** _____
**03** _____
**04** _____
**05** _____
**06** _____
**07** _____
**08** _____
**09** _____
**10** _____
**11** _____
**12** _____
**13** _____
**14** _____
**15** _____

## NOTES

_____
_____
_____
_____
_____

# DAILY MANIFEST

DATE:

## DAILY PRIORITIES

Give direction to your daily tasks - Write down what you want to achieve during the day and why it is important to you. Think long term - How are these things going to help you in 1 month, 6 months, or 1 year? If they won't, chances are, they're not that important.

**01**

**02**

**03**

## TO-DO LIST

Less important things to get done during the day. These might not be that strategic long term, but need to be done nevertheless.

01

02

03

04

05

06

07

08

09

10

11

12

13

14

15

## NOTES

# DAILY MANIFEST

DATE:

## DAILY PRIORITIES

Give direction to your daily tasks - Write down what you want to achieve during the day and why it is important to you. Think long term - How are these things going to help you in 1 month, 6 months, or 1 year? If they won't, chances are, they're not that important.

01
_____
_____
_____
_____
_____
_____

02
_____
_____
_____
_____
_____
_____

03
_____
_____
_____
_____
_____
_____

## TO-DO LIST

Less important things to get done during the day. These might not be that strategic long term, but need to be done nevertheless.

01 _____
02 _____
03 _____
04 _____
05 _____
06 _____
07 _____
08 _____
09 _____
10 _____
11 _____
12 _____
13 _____
14 _____
15 _____

## NOTES

_____
_____
_____
_____
_____
_____
_____

# DAILY MANIFEST

## DAILY PRIORITIES

Give direction to your daily tasks - Write down what you want to achieve during the day and why it is important to you. Think long term - How are these things going to help you in 1 month, 6 months, or 1 year? If they won't, chances are, they're not that important.

01
_____
_____
_____
_____
_____

02
_____
_____
_____
_____
_____

03
_____
_____
_____
_____
_____

## TO-DO LIST

Less important things to get done during the day. These might not be that strategic long term, but need to be done nevertheless.

01 _____
02 _____
03 _____
04 _____
05 _____
06 _____
07 _____
08 _____
09 _____
10 _____
11 _____
12 _____
13 _____
14 _____
15 _____

## NOTES

_____
_____
_____
_____
_____

# DAILY MANIFEST

DATE:

## DAILY PRIORITIES

Give direction to your daily tasks - Write down what you want to achieve during the day and why it is important to you. Think long term - How are these things going to help you in 1 month, 6 months, or 1 year? If they won't, chances are, they're not that important.

01
_____
_____
_____
_____
_____

02
_____
_____
_____
_____
_____

03
_____
_____
_____
_____
_____

## TO-DO LIST

Less important things to get done during the day. These might not be that strategic long term, but need to be done nevertheless.

01 _____
02 _____
03 _____
04 _____
05 _____
06 _____
07 _____
08 _____
09 _____
10 _____
11 _____
12 _____
13 _____
14 _____
15 _____

## NOTES

_____
_____
_____
_____
_____

# DAILY MANIFEST

DATE:

## DAILY PRIORITIES

Give direction to your daily tasks - Write down what you want to achieve during the day and why it is important to you. Think long term - How are these things going to help you in 1 month, 6 months, or 1 year? If they won't, chances are, they're not that important.

01
_____
_____
_____
_____
_____

02
_____
_____
_____
_____
_____

03
_____
_____
_____
_____
_____

## TO-DO LIST

Less important things to get done during the day. These might not be that strategic long term, but need to be done nevertheless.

01 _____
02 _____
03 _____
04 _____
05 _____
06 _____
07 _____
08 _____
09 _____
10 _____
11 _____
12 _____
13 _____
14 _____
15 _____

## NOTES

_____
_____
_____
_____
_____

# DAILY MANIFEST

## DAILY PRIORITIES

Give direction to your daily tasks - Write down what you want to achieve during the day and why it is important to you. Think long term - How are these things going to help you in 1 month, 6 months, or 1 year? If they won't, chances are, they're not that important.

01
_____
_____
_____
_____
_____

02
_____
_____
_____
_____
_____

03
_____
_____
_____
_____
_____

## TO-DO LIST

Less important things to get done during the day. These might not be that strategic long term, but need to be done nevertheless.

01 _____
02 _____
03 _____
04 _____
05 _____
06 _____
07 _____
08 _____
09 _____
10 _____
11 _____
12 _____
13 _____
14 _____
15 _____

## NOTES

_____
_____
_____
_____
_____

# DAILY MANIFEST

DATE:

## DAILY PRIORITIES

Give direction to your daily tasks - Write down what you want to achieve during the day and why it is important to you. Think long term - How are these things going to help you in 1 month, 6 months, or 1 year? If they won't, chances are, they're not that important.

01

02

03

## TO-DO LIST

Less important things to get done during the day. These might not be that strategic long term, but need to be done nevertheless.

01

02

03

04

05

06

07

08

09

10

11

12

13

14

15

## NOTES

# DAILY MANIFEST

DATE:

## DAILY PRIORITIES

Give direction to your daily tasks - Write down what you want to achieve during the day and why it is important to you. Think long term - How are these things going to help you in 1 month, 6 months, or 1 year? If they won't, chances are, they're not that important.

01

02

03

## TO-DO LIST

Less important things to get done during the day. These might not be that strategic long term, but need to be done nevertheless.

01

02

03

04

05

06

07

08

09

10

11

12

13

14

15

## NOTES

# DAILY MANIFEST

DATE:

## DAILY PRIORITIES

Give direction to your daily tasks - Write down what you want to achieve during the day and why it is important to you. Think long term - How are these things going to help you in 1 month, 6 months, or 1 year? If they won't, chances are, they're not that important.

01
_____
_____
_____
_____
_____

02
_____
_____
_____
_____
_____

03
_____
_____
_____
_____
_____

## TO-DO LIST

Less important things to get done during the day. These might not be that strategic long term, but need to be done nevertheless.

01 _____
02 _____
03 _____
04 _____
05 _____
06 _____
07 _____
08 _____
09 _____
10 _____
11 _____
12 _____
13 _____
14 _____
15 _____

## NOTES

_____
_____
_____
_____
_____

# DAILY MANIFEST

## DAILY PRIORITIES

Give direction to your daily tasks - Write down what you want to achieve during the day and why it is important to you. Think long term - How are these things going to help you in 1 month, 6 months, or 1 year? If they won't, chances are, they're not that important.

01
_____
_____
_____
_____
_____
_____

02
_____
_____
_____
_____
_____
_____

03
_____
_____
_____
_____
_____
_____

## TO-DO LIST

Less important things to get done during the day. These might not be that strategic long term, but need to be done nevertheless.

01 _____
02 _____
03 _____
04 _____
05 _____
06 _____
07 _____
08 _____
09 _____
10 _____
11 _____
12 _____
13 _____
14 _____
15 _____

## NOTES

_____
_____
_____
_____
_____
_____

# DAILY MANIFEST

DATE:

## DAILY PRIORITIES

Give direction to your daily tasks - Write down what you want to achieve during the day and why it is important to you. Think long term - How are these things going to help you in 1 month, 6 months, or 1 year? If they won't, chances are, they're not that important.

01
_____
_____
_____
_____
_____

02
_____
_____
_____
_____
_____

03
_____
_____
_____
_____
_____

## TO-DO LIST

Less important things to get done during the day. These might not be that strategic long term, but need to be done nevertheless.

01 _____
02 _____
03 _____
04 _____
05 _____
06 _____
07 _____
08 _____
09 _____
10 _____
11 _____
12 _____
13 _____
14 _____
15 _____

## NOTES

_____
_____
_____
_____
_____

# DAILY MANIFEST

## DAILY PRIORITIES

Give direction to your daily tasks - Write down what you want to achieve during the day and why it is important to you. Think long term - How are these things going to help you in 1 month, 6 months, or 1 year? If they won't, chances are, they're not that important.

01
_____
_____
_____
_____
_____
_____

02
_____
_____
_____
_____
_____
_____

03
_____
_____
_____
_____
_____
_____

## TO-DO LIST

Less important things to get done during the day. These might not be that strategic long term, but need to be done nevertheless.

01 _____
02 _____
03 _____
04 _____
05 _____
06 _____
07 _____
08 _____
09 _____
10 _____
11 _____
12 _____
13 _____
14 _____
15 _____

## NOTES

_____
_____
_____
_____
_____

# DAILY MANIFEST

DATE:

## DAILY PRIORITIES

Give direction to your daily tasks - Write down what you want to achieve during the day and why it is important to you. Think long term - How are these things going to help you in 1 month, 6 months, or 1 year? If they won't, chances are, they're not that important.

01

02

03

## TO-DO LIST

Less important things to get done during the day. These might not be that strategic long term, but need to be done nevertheless.

01

02

03

04

05

06

07

08

09

10

11

12

13

14

15

## NOTES

# DAILY MANIFEST

DATE:

## DAILY PRIORITIES

Give direction to your daily tasks - Write down what you want to achieve during the day and why it is important to you. Think long term - How are these things going to help you in 1 month, 6 months, or 1 year? If they won't, chances are, they're not that important.

01

02

03

## TO-DO LIST

Less important things to get done during the day. These might not be that strategic long term, but need to be done nevertheless.

01

02

03

04

05

06

07

08

09

10

11

12

13

14

15

## NOTES

# DAILY MANIFEST

DATE:

## DAILY PRIORITIES

Give direction to your daily tasks - Write down what you want to achieve during the day and why it is important to you. Think long term - How are these things going to help you in 1 month, 6 months, or 1 year? If they won't, chances are, they're not that important.

01

02

03

## TO-DO LIST

Less important things to get done during the day. These might not be that strategic long term, but need to be done nevertheless.

01

02

03

04

05

06

07

08

09

10

11

12

13

14

15

## NOTES

# NOTES

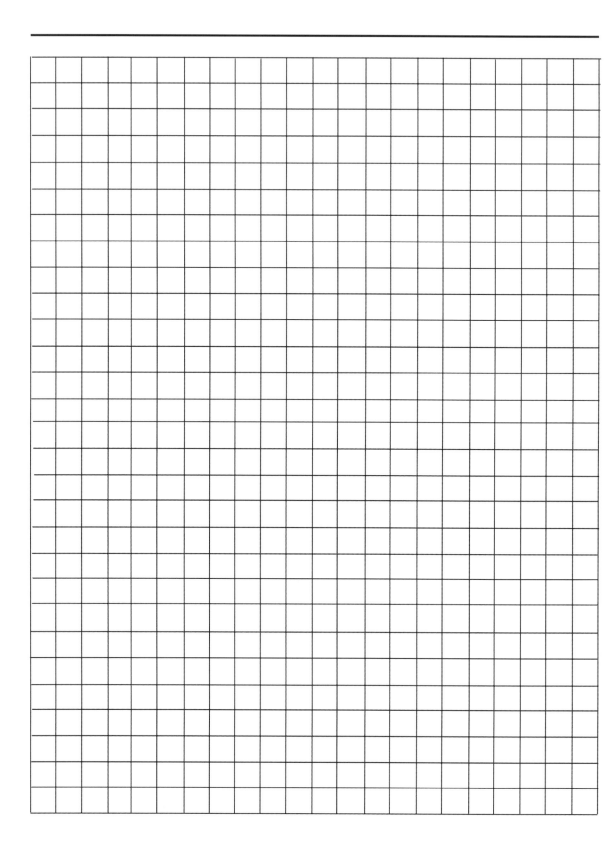

# NOTES

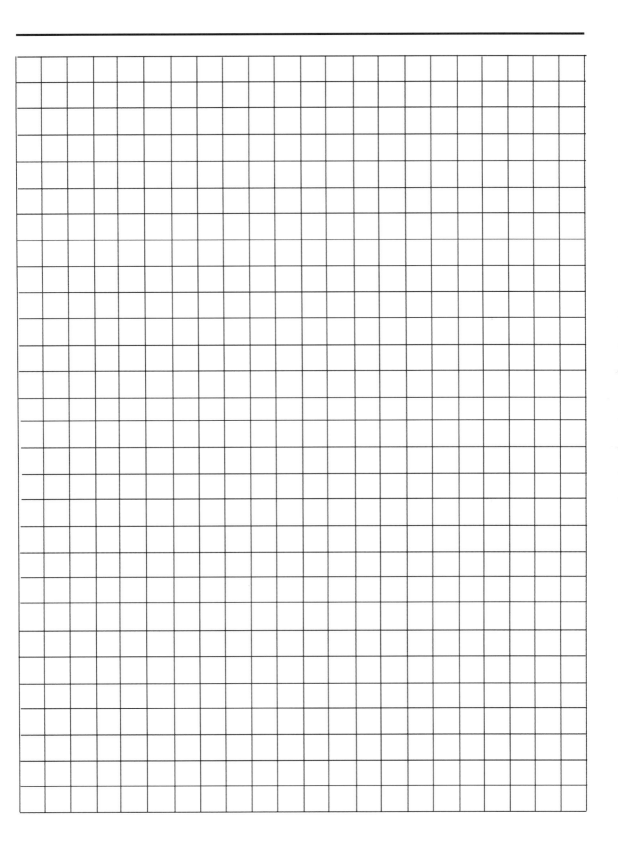

# NOTES

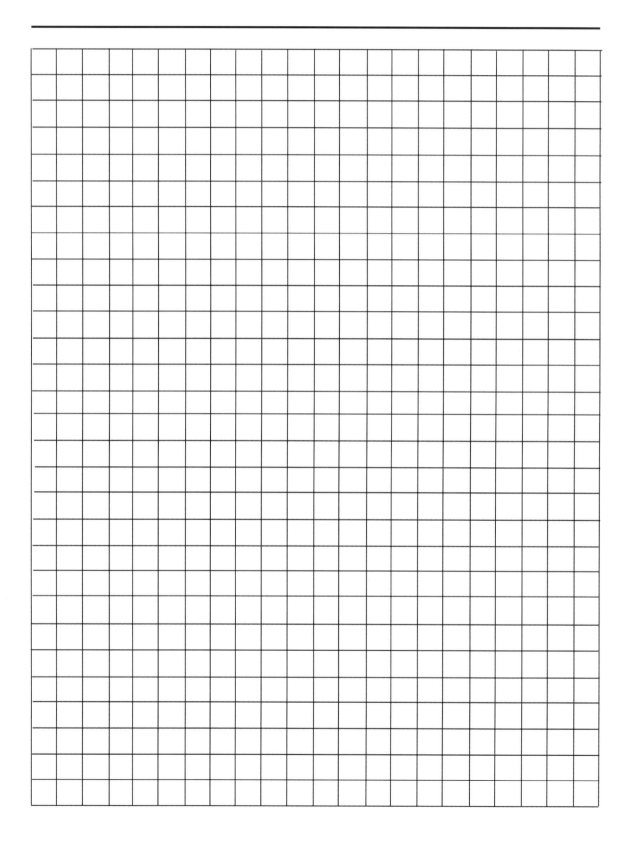

# NOTES

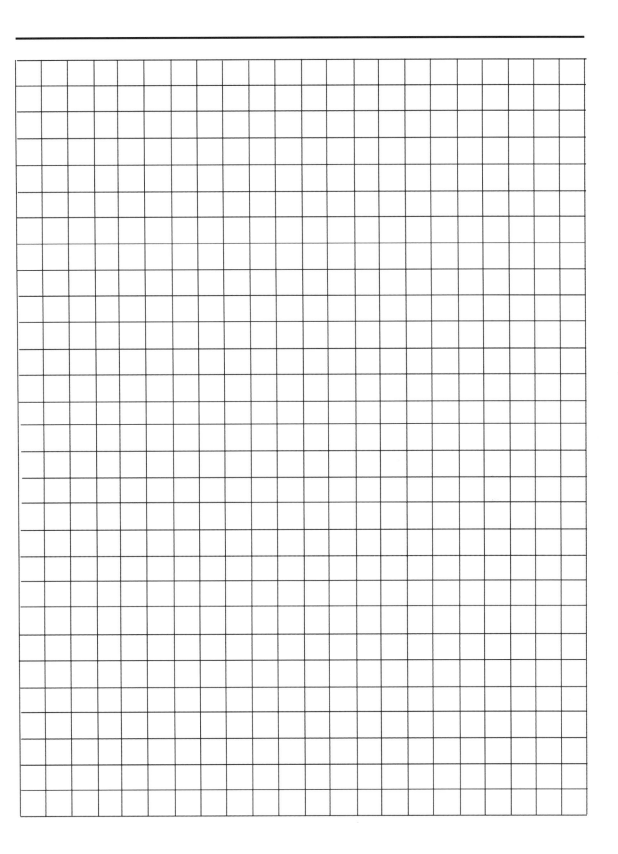

# NOTES

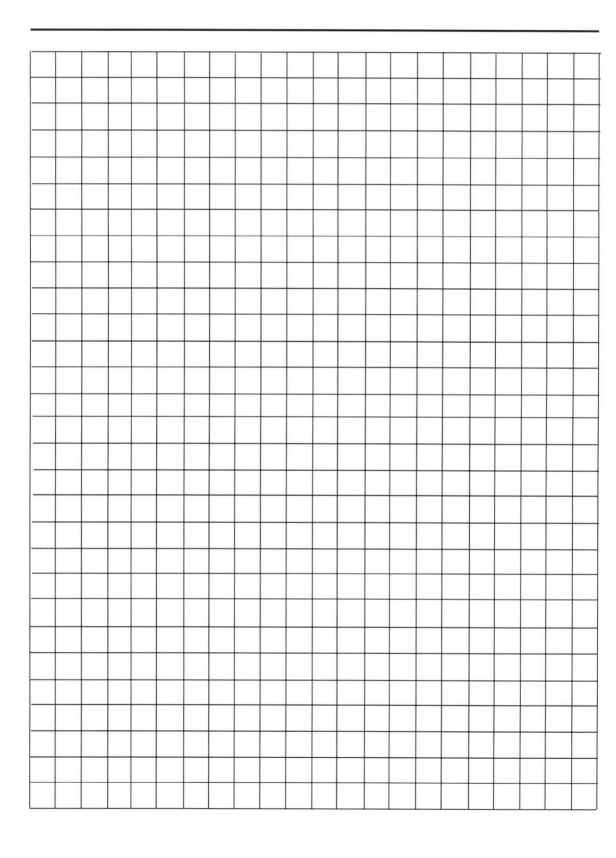

# NOTES

# NOTES

# NOTES

# NOTES

# NOTES

# NOTES

# NOTES

# NOTES

# NOTES

# NOTES

Made in the USA
Columbia, SC
22 February 2023

571ba472-e9fd-4e2b-96aa-b3ae0674531aR01